G000124176

ONE HELL OF A DAY

COCKTAILS TO FIX THAT SH*T

An Hachette UK Company
www.hachette.co.uk
First published in 2021 by Pyramid,
an imprint of Octopus Publishing Group Ltd
Carmelite House
50 Victoria Embankment
London, EC4Y 0DZ
www.octopusbooks.co.uk

ISBN: 978-0-7537-3463-6

A CIP catalogue record for this book is available from the British
Library

Printed and bound in China

10 9 8 7 6 5 4 3 2 1

Publisher: Lucy Pessell
Designer: Hannah Coughlin
Editor: Sarah Kennedy
Editorial Assistant: Emily Martin
Senior Production Controller: Emily Noto
Illustrations: TVZSU/Rawpixel.com

**This book contains cocktails made with raw or
lightly cooked eggs. It is prudent for more vulnerable
people to avoid uncooked or lightly cooked cocktails
made with eggs.**

ONE HELL OF A DAY

COCKTAILS TO FIX THAT SH*T

Vesper Rox

CONTENTS

BIG GUNS

MEASURES

The measure that has been used in the recipes is based on a bar jigger, which is 25 ml (1 fl oz).

If preferred, a different volume can be used, providing the proportions are kept constant within a drink and suitable adjustments are made to spoon measurements, where they occur.

Standard level spoon measurements are used in all recipes.

> 1 tablespoon = one 15 ml spoon (0.5 fl oz)
> 1 teaspoon = one 5 ml spoon (0.2 fl oz)

INTRODUCTION

"Alcohol is not the answer." Said someone who hasn't had the day you've just had.

"Not to get technical, but according to chemistry, alcohol is a solution." Said somone else. Find that someone and give them a high five.

This is a collection of nearly forty of the finest, friendliest and fiercest cocktails ever concocted that seem to have every type of bad day covered – in both name and spirit.

Loaded with Rescue Remedies to answer your prayers, and Big Guns to bring bad days to their knees, this is your handbook to sippable salvation. With swizzle sticks.

DEATH IN THE AFTERNOON

The seconds after lunch tick by, stretching into hours which feel like days. Seasons change. Years pass. You barely notice yourself atrophy, then mummify at your desk, before slowly turning to dust.

It's ok. This is called "the working week". Happens to us all.

A favourite of Ernest Hemmingway's, though to suggest Hemmingway had a favourite anything when it came to drinking possibly belies his zeal for the pastime. Approach this one with caution.

Makings:

½ measure absinthe

chilled Champagne, to top

The Fix:

Pour the absinthe into the bottom
of a Champagne flute, then carefully
add the Champagne.

No garnish.

GODFATHER

"Revenge is a dish best served cold."
Don Vito Corleone

"... in a glass, with amaretto and whisky."
Literally Everyone Else

A simple yet delicious snifter for whisky lovers. Amaretto's sweet almond flavour compliments the heather honey smoothness of Scottish whisky and really gets you in the mood for 70 years of vengeance and destruction.

Makings:

2 measures Scottish whisky

1 measure amaretto

The Fix:

Add both ingredients to a rocks glass
filled with ice and stir.

No garnish.

CORPSE REVIVER NO. 2

Is your job draining your vitality and eating your brains for breakfast? Have you trudged through your day, numb to the world? Here's a drink that packs a punch strong enough to bring any casualty of workplace drudgery back to the land of the living.

According to its creator (Harry Craddock) "four of these taken in quick succession will unrevive the corpse again." Start with one and see how you go.

Makings:

1 measure gin
1 measure lemon juice
1 measure Lillet Blanc
1 measure Cointreau
2 drops absinthe
lemon twist, to garnish

The Fix:

Add all the ingredients to your cocktail shaker.

Shake vigorously with cubed ice and double strain into a chilled coupette glass.

Garnish with a lemon twist.

ICEBERG

You don't have to go down with the ship.
Sink the f*cker.

A vodka rocks, enlivened with the slightest waft of absinthe. The brightness of the lime garnish will really bring you, and the drink, to life. Sally forth, Ice Queen.

Makings:

2 measures vodka

1 tsp absinthe (or Pernod)

lime, to garnish

The Fix:

Pour the vodka into an old-fashioned glass filled with cubed ice.

Add the absinthe, stir briefly and garnish with a lime twist.

ZOMBIE

I just remember the clawing hands, the screams. The dreadful screams. Hordes of wild and wide-eyed scavengers arrived. I ran.

F*cking Happy Hour.

This is a fearsomely potent rum punch, so potent in fact that in most reputable cocktail bars' customers would usually be restricted to just one of them. Do be careful.

Makings:

1½ measures light rum

1½ measures dark rum

½ measure Velvet Falernum

½ measure overproof rum

¾ measure lime juice

½ measure grenadine

2 measures grapefruit juice

2 dashes absinthe

1 dash Angostura bitters

lime, cocktail cherries, mint to garnish

The Fix:

Add all the ingredients to your cocktail shaker, shake vigorously and strain into a hurricane glass (or tiki mug if you have one) filled with crushed ice.

Garnish extravagantly with lime slices, cocktail cherries, mint sprigs and anything else you like.

SURFACE TO AIR

"The missiles come first, and the justifications come second."
E. P. Thompson

Sounds reasonable.

A coconut daiquiri, with incoming hints of tropical pineapple and explosive mint. Apparently devised in the bath by London bartender of note Liam Cotter at Highwater, Dalston in 2015.

Makings:

1 measure coconut rum

1 measure gin

¾ measure lime juice

½ measure fresh pineapple juice

½ measure sugar syrup

8 mint leaves

The Fix:

Add all the ingredients to your cocktail shaker, shake vigorously and double strain into a chilled coupette glass.

No garnish.

BREAKFAST MARTINI

Some days start shouting at you before you're even out of bed.

Here is your answer to that.

A modern classic, created in 1996 at the Lanesborough Hotel, London. The inspiration for Salvatore Calabrese's witty riff on the White Lady cocktail was said to have come to him at breakfast. Salvatore, we feel you. And thank you.

Makings:

1¾ measures gin

½ measure Cointreau

¾ measure lemon juice

1 tsp orange marmalade

orange and toast (optional), to garnish

The Fix:

Add all the ingredients to your cocktail shaker and give the liquid a quick stir to break up the marmalade.

Shake vigorously with cubed ice and double strain into a chilled martini glass.

Garnish with an orange twist and, (bit random), a small slice of toast.

HARVEY WALLBANGER

One for the nights the neighbours just won't stop.

Probably known more for its name than its ingredients, the Harvey Wallbanger is something of a forgotten jewel of the 1970s. Like avocado bathroom suites. But shinier and more precious.

Makings:

1½ measures vodka

½ measure Galliano

5 measures fresh orange juice

orange, to garnish

The Fix:

Add the vodka and orange juice
to a hurricane or highball glass filled
with ice.

Stir, and then float the Galliano over
the top.

Garnish with a slice of orange.

PENICILLIN

Mediiiiic!

Alexander Fleming did an okay job of Penicillin, but Sam Ross of the pioneering New York cocktail spot Milk & Honey took things to the next level. Go easy on this one. We're aiming for cure, not kill.

Makings:

2 measures Scottish whisky

1 measure lemon juice

½ measure honey syrup

½ measure ginger syrup

2 tbsp Islay whisky (smoky or peated)

The Fix:

Combine the Scotch, lemon juice and syrup in a cocktail shaker.

Shake with ice.

Strain over fresh ice into an old-fashioned glass.

Float the Islay whisky over the top.

KIWI SMASH

Until we can be sure that kiwifruits have feelings too, you're ok taking a shovel to them in the name of catharsis.

If you don't have a shovel to hand, a spoon will do the job.

A citric envy-green vodka Fix. With smashing.

Makings:

2 measures vodka

¾ measure lime juice

½ measure sugar syrup

1 kiwifruit, peeled and cubed

lime, to garnish

The Fix:

Drop the kiwifruit into a rocks glass, and muddle with a spoon.

Add the remaining ingredients, fill the glass with crushed ice and churn.

Top with more crushed ice and garnish with a lime wedge.

SCREWDRIVER

Feeling like you've come off your hinges,
or a couple of screws have come loose?
A few nails short of a bucket?

Down tools. Up drink.

*No amount of waffle will mask the simple fact
that this is vodka mixed with orange juice, but
its position as a cultural icon is indisputable
and it does the job nicely.*

Makings:

2 measures vodka

5 measures fresh orange juice

orange, to garnish

The Fix:

Add the ingredients to a highball glass filled with ice.

Stir, and garnish with a slice of orange.

ARMY AND NAVY

Your personal space has been breached one too many times today.

Scurry back to your bunker and call in the military. This one has your back.

A gin sour; flavoured with almond. This can be fiendishly difficult to balance, so ensure you measure your ingredients accurately and shake well. Or pay no heed to the measures and have a jolly nice time anyway.

Makings:

2 measures gin

1 measure lemon juice

½ measure orgeat syrup

lemon twist, to garnish

The Fix:

Add all the ingredients to your cocktail shaker.

Shake vigorously with cubed ice and double strain into a chilled coupette glass.

Garnish with a lemon twist.

OLD PAL

"A friend in need is a friend indeed."

And there's no better friend than an old pal bearing whiskey, vermouth and Campari in times of need.

A bracing dry Manhattan, with a strong bitter element provided by Campari. Said to have originated in Paris in the 1920s at Harry's New York Bar.

Makings:

1½ measures rye whiskey

¾ measure dry vermouth

½ measure Campari

lemon twist, to garnish

The Fix:

Add all the ingredients to a cocktail shaker or mixing glass filled with cubed ice.

Stir for 30 seconds and strain into a chilled martini glass.

Garnish with a twist of lemon.

HURRICANE

Channel your inner wolf, and huff and puff and blow that shit down.

Strong and sweet, and immortalized at Pat O'Brien's bar in New Orleans, this is a tropical storm of a punch, with rich fruit whirling around with sharp citrus and strong gusts of rum.

Makings:

1½ measures white rum
1½ measures dark rum
1 measure lime juice
¾ measure passionfruit syrup
2 tsp grenadine
½ measure orange juice
½ measure pineapple juice
orange slice, cocktail cherry to garnish

The Fix:

Add all ingredients to your cocktail shaker, shake vigorously and strain into a hurricane glass filled with cubed ice.
Garnish with an orange slice and a cocktail cherry.

FOG CUTTER

The perfect tipple if you're hoping to shed new light and get a different perspective on things.

Trader Vic said it best: "Fog Cutter, hell. After two of these, you won't even see the stuff."

Richly flavoured and wickedly strong, this complex rum punch is a Tiki classic. Its origins are as foggy as its name suggests but what is certain is that too many of them will have you on the floor. Quaff carefully.

Makings:

1 measure light rum

1 measure Cognac

½ measure gin

½ measure sherry

½ measure orgeat

¾ measure lemon juice

2 measures orange juice

orange slice, to garnish

The Fix:

Add all the ingredients to your cocktail shaker, shake and strain into an old-fashioned glass filled with cubed ice.

Garnish with an orange slice.

RUSTY NAIL

Harbingers of tetanus, gangrene and amputation, rusty nails are a subtle menace to have in the arsenal.

... or failing that, Scotch and Drambuie works too.

A Scottish classic, around since the 1940s and the perfect cocktail for a whisky lover or scrap merchant. Drambuie is a whisky-based herb and honey liqueur, so you are stirring whisky into whisky. You are winning.

Makings:

2 measures Scottish whisky

1 measure Drambuie

lemon twist, to garnish

The Fix:

Add both ingredients to an old-fashioned glass filled with cubed ice.

Stir briefly, and garnish with a lemon twist.

THE FIX

There is literally nothing gin won't fix.

The simplest of Sours, and really the very building blocks of all drinks making – first recorded in Jerry Thomas's How to Mix Drinks *(1862). Gin can be substituted for a different spirit. Though why you'd want to do that is perplexing.*

Makings:

2 measures gin

1 measure lemon juice

¾ measure sugar syrup

seasonal fruit, to garnish

The Fix:

Add the ingredients to a rocks glass filled with crushed ice.

Churn, and garnish with seasonal fruit of your choosing.

COMBINED FORCES

"We are stronger together than we are alone."
Walter Payton

True. And with Triple Sec for an ally, a martini is going to win the war.

An elegant vodka martini and a fantastic alternative to gin as a pre-dinner aperitif or pre-battle starter.

Makings:

2 measures vodka

½ measure Triple Sec

½ measure dry vermouth

2 dashes orange bitters

lemon twist, to garnish

The Fix:

Add all the ingredients to a cocktail shaker or mixing glass, and fill with cubed ice.

Stir for 30 seconds, and strain into a chilled martini glass.

Garnish with a lemon twist.

HANKY PANKY

There's very little some hanky panky won't fix. And even less that a quick session with some gin, vermouth and Fernet Branca can't sort.

A subtle twist on the Martinez cocktail, created by Ada Coleman at the Savoy Hotel, London, in the early 1900s. Fernet Branca is an intensely bitter Italian amaro, and cuts through the sweetness of the vermouth superbly. Worth a try.

Makings:

2 measures gin

1 measure sweet vermouth

1 tbsp Fernet Branca

orange twist, to garnish

The Fix:

Add all the ingredients to a cocktail shaker or mixing glass, and fill with cubed ice.

Stir for 30 seconds, and strain into a chilled martini glass.

Garnish with an orange twist.

FRENCH 75

The field gun of choice for the French in World War I, French 75's had a habit of blowing away everything they came into contact with.

See that pile of laundry over there?
Ready, aim, fire! See? Gone.

Created at Harry's New York Bar in Paris in 1915, this is as much a Tom Collins with a Champagne top as it is anything else. The rapid artillery fire of the bubbles is lovely.

Makings:

1 measure gin
½ measure lemon juice
½ measure sugar syrup
chilled Champagne, to top
lemon twist, to garnish

The Fix:

Shake the gin, lemon juice and sugar syrup vigorously and strain into a Champagne flute.

Top with Champagne and garnish with a lemon twist.

RUDE COSMOPOLITAN

Sink back into the sofa and relax – the day is done.

While away a few hours thinking up insults for purveyors of avocado toast, matcha tea and washi tape.

A Cosmopolitan made with tequila. Or a Margarita made with cranberry juice. It'd be rude not to try it.

Makings:

1½ measures tequila

1 measure Cointreau

1 measure cranberry juice

½ measure lime juice

lime wedge dusted in sea salt, to garnish

The Fix:

Add all the ingredients to your cocktail shaker, shake vigorously and double strain into a chilled coupette glass.

Garnish with a lime wedge dusted in sea salt.

STINGER

A "stinger" can refer to a short, sharp punch to the head, or sudden pain in the neck.

This, and the fact it's made of Cognac and crème de menthe, makes it the perfect drink to serve to an enemy.

A "stinging", mint-laced cocktail from Harry Craddock, first published in The Savoy Cocktail Book *(1930). It was apparently popular with US Airmen but whether that was before or after missions is unclear.*

Makings:

2 measures Cognac

½ measure crème de menthe

mint leaf, to garnish

The Fix:

Add all the ingredients to your cocktail shaker, shake vigorously and double strain into a chilled martini glass.

Garnish with a mint leaf.

SBAGLIATO

So maybe you left your keys, or your phone, or your child, or all three, in that shop you left an hour ago. And maybe you've only just remembered.

Relax. Everyone makes mistakes.

"Sbagliato" in Italian roughly translates as "a mistake". According to cocktail lore, the Sbagliato was created when a busy bartender in Milan poured Prosecco instead of gin while preparing a Negroni. Which just goes to show that we shouldn't get so hung up on our mistakes all the time.

Makings:

1 measure Campari

1 measure sweet vermouth

2 measures chilled Prosecco

orange slice, to garnish

The Fix:

Add the ingredients to a rocks glass filled with cubed ice, stir briefly and garnish with a slice of orange.

WHITE LADY

If you can't get even in this life, just come back and haunt them.

Essentially a Sidecar made with gin, argument raged between Harry McElhone and Harry Craddock as to who created this evergreen classic. One assumes they continued the fight into the afterlife.

Makings:

1½ measures gin

1 measure Cointreau

¾ measure lemon juice

lemon twist, to garnish

The Fix:

Add all the ingredients to your cocktail shaker, shake vigorously and double strain into a chilled coupette glass.

Garnish with a lemon twist.

HEMINGWAY DAIQUIRI

"I drink to make other people more interesting."
Ernest Hemingway

This is sound advice. And a couple of these will render the watercooler crew nothing short of fascinating.

Created at Floridita in Havana for erstwhile barfly Ernest Hemingway – whose penchant for Daiquiris was only inhibited by his unusually sour palate – the Hemingway Daiquiri is lip curlingly sour, so do add a touch more sugar if you wish.

Makings:

1¾ measures light rum

¾ measure Maraschino

1 measure lime juice

1 measure grapefruit juice

2 tsp sugar syrup

lime wedge, to garnish

The Fix:

Add all the ingredients to your cocktail shaker, shake vigorously and double strain into a chilled coupette glass.

Garnish with a lime wedge on the side of the glass.

GUNFIRE

Start the day as you mean to go on and enter battle mode.

Served to troops as a form of dutch courage before mounting morning attacks, who doesn't love the sound of gunfire in the morning?

A cup of tea, made all the more palatable by a glug of rum. And that's it. There wasn't much call for bartenders on the front lines.

Makings:

1 measure rum

black tea

The Fix:

Make a cup of strong black tea and add the rum.

ESPRESSO MARTINI

Morning has broken. It's just not working.

When asked by a customer to make a drink that would "wake me up, and f*ck me up", London bartender of note Dick Bradsell made this.

Morning is fixed.

A modern classic and bad-day breakfast staple. If you're not too far gone and care for such things, for the desired foam, you must shake vigorously for a good 10 seconds, and ensure your coffee is of the best quality available. A foamless affair with instant granules will work too.

Makings:

1½ measures vodka

1 measure coffee liqueur

1 measure fresh espresso coffee

½ measure sugar syrup

3 coffee beans, to garnish

The Fix:

Add all the ingredients to your cocktail shaker.

Shake vigorously and double strain into a chilled martini glass.

Garnish with the coffee beans.

SATAN'S WHISKERS

If cat whiskers bestow luck upon the owner then Satan's whiskers will bestow upon the drinker the power to seduce all of mankind into temptation and drag them into the raging fires of hell.

How will you spend Saturday night?

Conceived by Harry Craddock, first published in The Savoy Cocktail Book. *A richer take on the Bronx cocktail, wickedly named and sharp to the taste.*

Makings:

1½ measures gin

½ measure orange Curaçao

½ measure sweet vermouth

½ measure dry vermouth

1½ measures orange juice

2 dashes orange bitters

The Fix:

Add all the ingredients to your cocktail shaker, shake vigorously and double strain into a chilled coupette glass.

No garnish.

BLOODY MARY

If a tomato-based vodka drink that can both revive your spirits and invoke the spirit of Mary Tudor when its name is called into a mirror can't brighten the day ahead, I'm not sure we have any more to say to each other.

The Bloody Mary is quite rightly a wholly subjective drinking experience that varies from one person to another – the only staples being vodka and tomato juice. The recipe here is a useful starting point, but all seasoning and spicing can and should be adjusted to taste.

Makings:

2 measures vodka

5 measures tomato juice

½ measure lemon juice

4 dashes Worcestershire sauce

2 dashes tabasco sauce

1 tbsp horseradish cream

pinch of salt

pinch of cracked black pepper

celery stick, lemon wedge, green olives to garnish

The Fix:

Add all the ingredients to a highball glass, stirring in cubed ice as you go.

Garnish with a celery stick, lemon wedge and green olives.

BLOOD AND SAND

Blood and Sand is a 1922 film starring Rudolf Valentino as a bull fighter.

The message here is: today is the day to take the bull by the horns. And to leave it there, as (spoiler alert) you'll end up in a toxic relationship with Rita Hayworth and die.

One of the few classic cocktails to feature Scotch, this is sweet, strong (and sacrilegious to some).

Makings:

1 measure Scottish whisky

1 measure sweet vermouth

1 measure cherry brandy

1 measure orange juice (freshly squeezed)

orange twist to garnish

The Fix:

Add all the ingredients to a cocktail shaker or mixing glass, and fill with cubed ice.

Stir briefly and strain into a chilled martini glass.

Garnish with an orange twist.

SOUTH OF THE BORDER

When things go south, drink tequila.

A snappy tequila sipper, sitting somewhere between an Old Fashioned and an Espresso Martini — sharp and sweet, coffee-laced agave goodness.

Makings:

2 measures tequila

¾ measure Kahlúa

The Fix:

Add both ingredients to an old-
fashioned glass filled with cubed ice
and stir briefly.

No garnish.

SOUTHSIDE

"Don't mistake my kindness for weakness. I am kind to everyone, but when someone is unkind to me, weak is not what you are going to remember about me."
Al Capone

Be more Al tomorrow. But less criminal.

Favoured by Al Capone, the Southside was most likely a product of Prohibition, when flavourings and sweeteners were required to mask the rough edges of poorly made "bathtub" gin. Fresh and lively. Like Capone's attitude to racketeering and fraud.

Makings:

2 measures gin

¾ measure lime juice

¾ measure sugar syrup

6 mint leaves

mint, to garnish

The Fix:

Add all the ingredients to your
cocktail shaker, shake vigorously
and double strain into a chilled
coupette glass.

Garnish with a mint leaf.

HANGMAN'S BLOOD

Although actual hangman's blood is scarce in grocery stores these days, a pint of this might be just as restorative.

Anthony Burgess insists this (his own take on the recipe) "tastes very smooth, induces a somewhat metaphysical elation, and rarely leaves a hangover."

We implore you to drink responsibly.

Makings:

2 measures gin

2 measures whisky

2 measures dark rum

2 measures port

2 measures brandy

1 small bottle of stout

Champagne, to top

The Fix:

Add all of the ingredients to a pint glass and then pour in the stout.

Top with Champagne.

B-52

This subsonic shot is guaranteed to blow your problems sky-high, at least until the morning.

In Canada, a popular riff on the B-52 is made with whiskey in place of the Grand Marnier and is known as ... a Duck Fart. If duck farts float your up-and-at-'em boat, good for you.

Makings:

½ measure Kahlúa

½ measure Baileys Irish Cream

½ measure Grand Marnier

The Fix:

Pour the Kahlúa into a shot glass.

Slowly and carefully pour the Baileys into the glass over the back of a spoon (preferably a bar spoon) so it floats atop the Kahlúa.

Carefully pour the Grand Marnier into the glass using the same layering method.

No garnish.

UESPER

If you're James Bond, this is one to help you concentrate on how to infiltrate and destroy an organization or bankrupt some special agents.

If you're anyone else, it's one to help you complete a job application or decipher your bank statement.

The only truly acceptable occasion when a Martini is shaken – and derived straight from the pages of Ian Fleming's first James Bond novel, Casino Royale *(1953).*

Makings:

2½ measures gin

1 measure vodka

½ measure Lillet Blanc

lemon twist, to garnish

The Fix:

Add all the ingredients to the bottom of your cocktail shaker, and fill the top-half of it with ice.

Shake vigorously and double strain into a chilled martini glass.

Garnish with a lemon twist.

GIMLET

"Some days I feel like playing it smooth.
Some days I feel like playing it like a
waffle iron."
Raymond Chandler

Try playing tomorrow like a waffle iron.

*The recipe for the Gimlet varies from source
to source, with Raymond Chandler calling
for just lime cordial, others for fresh lime and
a touch of sugar syrup. We've attempted a
compromise.*

Makings:

2½ measures gin

½ measure lime cordial

½ measure lime juice

lime twist, to garnish

The Fix:

Add all the ingredients to your
cocktail shaker, shake vigorously and
strain into a chilled coupette glass.

Garnish with a lime twist.

DIRTY MARTINI

"If you can't fix it without duct tape or a martini, it ain't worth fixing."
Unknown

"Happiness is … finding two olives in your martini when you're hungry."
Johnny Carson

Don't worry; be happy.

Apparently a creation of none other than President Franklin Delano Roosevelt – the dry saltiness of the Dirty Martini is loathed and loved in equal measure, depending on the drinker's feelings about olives.
Delicious. Or awful.

Makings:

2½ measures vodka

¼ measure dry vermouth

½ measure olive brine

olives, to garnish

The Fix:

Add all the ingredients to a cocktail shaker or mixing glass, and fill with cubed ice.

Stir for 30 seconds, and strain into a chilled martini glass.

Garnish with olives.

FIGHTING BOB

Everyone knows Bob.

Bob? Oh yeah, I know Bob. Salt of the Earth. Fighting the good fight. Good old Bob.

Get Bob in your corner.

A dry, herbaceous and punchy yet sophisticated highball, this will keep you on your toes and off the ropes through all 12 rounds.

Makings:

1 measure gin
½ measure Chartreuse
½ measure cherry brandy
¼ measure lemon juice
1 dash Angostura bitters
soda water, to taste
cocktail cherries, to garnish

The Fix:

Add all the ingredients to a highball
glass filled with cubed ice, stir briefly
and garnish with cocktail cherries.

BAR BASICS AND TECHNIQUES

WHAT MAKES A GOOD COCKTAIL

Good cocktails, like good food, are based around quality ingredients. As with cooking, using fresh and homemade ingredients can often make the huge difference between a good drink and an outstanding drink. All of this can be found in department stores, online or in kitchen shops.

COCKTAIL INGREDIENTS

Ice

This is a key part of cocktails and you'll need lots of it. Purchase it from your supermarket, or freeze big tubs of water, then crack this up to use in your drinks. If you're hosting a big party and want to serve some punches, which will need lots of ice, it may be worthwhile finding if you have a local ice supplier that supplies catering companies, as this can be much more cost-effective.

Citrus juice

It's important to use fresh citrus juice in your drinks; bottled versions taste awful and will not produce good drinks.

Store your fruit out of the refrigerator at room temperature. Look for a soft-skinned fruit for juicing, which you can do with a juicer or citrus press. You can keep fresh citrus juice for a couple of days in the refrigerator, sealed to prevent oxidation.

Sugar syrup

You can buy sugar syrup or you can make your own. The most basic form of sugar syrup is made by mixing caster sugar and hot water together, and stirring until the sugar has dissolved. The key when preparing sugar syrups is to use a 1:1 ratio of sugar to liquid. White sugar acts as a flavour enhancer, while dark sugars have unique, more toffee flavours and work well with dark spirits.

Basic sugar syrup recipe

(Makes 1 litre (1¾ pints) of sugar syrup)

1. Dissolve 1 kg (2 lb) caster sugar in 1 litre (1¾ pints) of hot water.
2. Allow to cool.

Sugar syrup will keep in a sterilized bottle stored in the refrigerator for up to two weeks.

CHOOSING GLASSWARE

There are many different cocktails, but they all fall into one of three categories: long, short or shot. Long drinks generally have more mixer than alcohol, often served with ice and a straw. The terms "straight up" and "on the rocks" are synonymous with the short drink, which tends to be more about the spirit, often combined with a single mixer at most. Finally, there is the shot which is made up mainly from spirits and liqueurs, designed to give a quick hit of alcohol. Glasses are tailored to the type of drinks they will contain.

Champagne flute

Used for Champagne or Champagne cocktails, the narrow mouth of the flute helps the drink to stay fizzy.

Champagne saucer

A classic glass, but not very practical for serving Champagne as the drink quickly loses its fizz.

Margarita or Coupette glass

When used for a Margarita, the rim is dipped in salt. Also used for daiquiris and other fruit-based cocktails.

Highball glass

Suitable for any long cocktail, such as a Long Island Iced Tea.

Collins glass

This is similar to a highball glass but is slightly narrower.

Wine glass

Sangria is often served in one, but they are not usually used for cocktails.

Old-Fashioned glass

Also known as a rocks glass, this is great for any drink that's served on the rocks or straight up.

Shot glass

Often found in two sizes — for a single or double measure. They are ideal for a single mouthful.

Balloon glass

Often used for fine spirits. The glass can be warmed to encourage the release of the drink's aroma.

Hurricane glass

Mostly found in beach bars, used for creamy, rum-based drinks.

Boston glass

Often used by bartenders for mixing cocktails, good for fruity drinks.

Toddy glass

A toddy glass is generally used for a hot drink, such as Irish Coffee.

Sling glass

This has a very short stemmed base and is most famously used for a Singapore Sling.

Martini glass

Also known as a cocktail glass, its thin-neck design makes sure your hand can't warm the glass or the cocktail.

USEFUL EQUIPMENT

Shaker

The Boston shaker is the most simple option, but it needs to be used in conjunction with a hawthorne strainer. Alternatively you could choose a shaker with a built-in strainer.

Measure or jigger

Single and double measures are available and are essential when you are mixing ingredients so that the proportions are always the same. One measure is 25 ml or 1 fl oz.

Mixing glass

A mixing glass is used for those drinks that require only a gentle stirring before they are poured or strained.

Hawthorne strainer

This type of strainer is often used in conjunction with a Boston shaker, but a simple tea strainer will also work well.

Bar spoon

Similar to a teaspoon but with a long handle, a bar spoon is used for stirring, layering and muddling drinks.

Muddling stick

Similar to a pestle, which will work just as well, a muddling stick, or muddler, is used to crush fruit or herbs in a glass or shaker for drinks like the Mojito.

Bottle opener

Choose a bottle opener with two attachments, one for metal-topped bottles and a corkscrew for wine bottles.

Pourers

A pourer is inserted into the top of a spirit bottle to enable the spirit to flow in a controlled manner.

Food processor

A food processor or blender is useful for making frozen cocktails and smoothies.

Equipment for garnishing

Exotic drinks may be prettified with a paper umbrella and several long drinks are served with straws or swizzle sticks.

TECHNIQUES

With just a few basic techniques, your bartending skills will be complete. Follow the instructions to hone your craft.

Blending

Frozen cocktails and smoothies are blended with ice in a blender until they are of a smooth consistency. Be careful not to add too much ice as this will dilute the cocktail. It's best to add a little at a time.

Shaking

The best-known cocktail technique and probably the most common. Used to mix ingredients thoroughly and quickly, and to chill the drink before serving.

1. Half-fill a cocktail shaker with ice cubes, or cracked or crushed ice.
2. If the recipe calls for a chilled glass add a few ice cubes and some cold water to the glass, swirl it around and discard.

3. Add the ingredients to the shaker and shake until a frost forms on the outside.
4. Strain the cocktail into the glass and serve.

Muddling

A technique used to bring out the flavours of herbs and fruit using a blunt tool called a muddler.

1. Add chosen herb(s) to a highball glass. Add some sugar syrup and some lime wedges.
2. Hold the glass firmly and use a muddler or pestle to twist and press down.
3. Continue for 30 seconds, top up with crushed ice and add remaining ingredients.

Double-straining

To prevent all traces of puréed fruit and ice fragments from entering the glass, use a shaker with a built-in strainer in conjunction with a hawthorne strainer. A fine strainer also works well.

Layering

Some spirits can be served layered on top of each other, causing lighter spirits to float on top of your cocktail.

1. Pour the first ingredient into a glass, taking care that it does not touch the sides.
2. Position a bar spoon in the centre of the glass, rounded part down and facing you. Rest the spoon against the side of the glass as your pour the second ingredient down the spoon. It should float on top of the first liquid.
3. Repeat with the third ingredient, then carefully remove the spoon.

Stirring

Used when the ingredients need to be mixed and chilled, but also maintain their clarity. This ensures there are no ice fragments or air bubbles throughout the drink. Some cocktails require the ingredients to be prepared in a mixing glass, then strained into the serving glass.

1. Add ingredients to a glass, in recipe order.

2. Use a bar spoon to stir the drink, lightly or vigorously, as described in the recipe.

3. Finish the drink with any decoration and serve.